Seeing

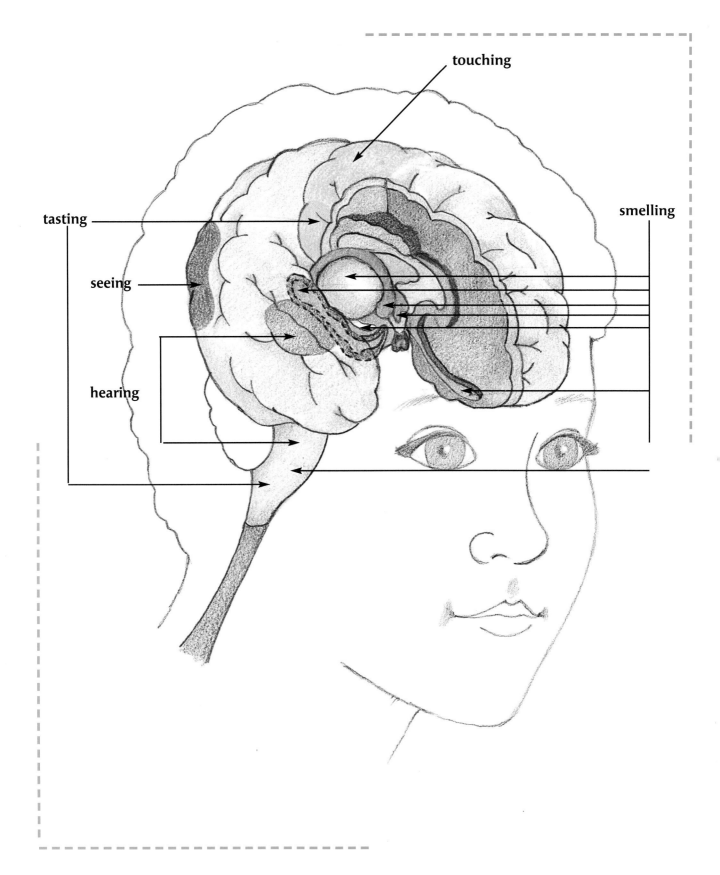

touching

smelling

tasting

seeing

hearing

Seeing

Dr. Alvin Silverstein, Virginia Silverstein,
and Laura Silverstein Nunn

Senses and Sensors
Twenty-First Century Books
Brookfield, Connecticut

Photographs courtesy of Photo Researchers, Inc.: pp. 8 (© Phil Jude/SPL), 11 (© David Parker/SPL), 20 (© Ralph C. Eagle, Jr., M.D.), 23 (both, © Leonard Lessin, FBPA), 24 (both © Ralph C. Eagle, Jr., M.D.), 43 (© 1998 Gregory G. Dimijian), 50 (© Ken Cavanagh), 53 (© Geoff Tompkinson/SPL); Peter Arnold, Inc.: pp. 13 (© Fred Bavendam), 35 (© Leonard Lessin); Phototake: pp. 15 (© Dr. Dennis Kunkel), 26 (© Rosebush Vision), 37 (both © Gerry Davis), 38 (© Mark Maio); The Image Works: pp. 32 (© Fujifotos), 46 (© Network Productions), 48 (© Abe Rezny/TIW) Illustrations by Anne Canevari Green

Library of Congress Cataloging-in-Publication Data
Silverstein, Alvin
Seeing / by Alvin Silverstein, Virginia Silverstein and Laura Silverstein Nunn.
p. cm. — (Senses and sensors)
Includes bibliographical references and index.
ISBN 0-7613-1663-9 (lib. bdg.)
1. Vision—Juvenile literature. [1. Vision. 2. Eye. 3. Senses and sensation.] I. Nunn, Laura Silverstein. II. Title. III. Series.
QP475.7 .S54 2001
612.8'4—dc21
2001018092

Published by Twenty-First Century Books
A Division of The Millbrook Press, Inc.
2 Old New Milford Road
Brookfield, Connecticut 06804
www.millbrookpress.com

Contents

Seeing

Do you recognize the objects in this photograph?
Whether we are looking at a picturesque sunset, a speeding
car, a colorful rainbow, or a slimy frog, the messages
from our eyes are interpreted by our brain and turned
into meaningful perceptions of the world.

one
Pictures of the world

We can recognize friends right away from just a brief glimpse of their faces or even by watching them walk in the distance. We can distinguish millions of shades of color. We can identify cars, animals, trees, flowers, and many other things by their shapes, even if we just see their outlines. Looking at objects, we can guess whether they will be hard or soft, rough or smooth. Usually we can also tell how close or far away things are, although sometimes we may be fooled. Everything we know about the world comes through our five main senses—sight, smell, taste, hearing, and touch. In this book we will focus on seeing, the sense of **vision**.

All living organisms—humans, animals, and even plants—have senses. They gather information about the world through specialized structures called **sensors**. These sensors detect various types of energy and send information about them to the brain to be translated into meaningful messages.

Some animals have senses more acute than our own. What would it be like, for example, if you could see while walking through a dark room? Or what if you could read an eye chart from more than a mile away? Some animals can do things like that: A cat can spot a scurrying mouse under very low-light conditions that would seem dark to us, and a soaring eagle can see a field mouse on the ground a mile away.

People have developed devices—artificial sensors—to expand our senses to equal or even surpass those of animals. Using infrared goggles we can see in the dark, and telescopes help us to see as far as the stars!

two
Seeing light

What do you see when you are reading a book? You might say it looks like pages of printed words. Actually, what you are really seeing is light. When you look at an object, such as a book, light is **reflected** or mirrored back to your eyes. The light that enters your eyes forms a pattern of light rays, which are detected by specialized sensors and then turned into signals that travel on nerves, to be interpreted by the brain.

What Is Light?

Light is a form of energy. Sunlight is our most powerful form of light energy. When sunlight shines on the earth, it moves like waves through water. But light energy does not need to travel through a medium (substance) like water. In fact, light moves freely through the near-vacuum of outer space.

The light that we see is called white light or **visible light**. White light is really made up of a variety of colors—red, orange, yellow, green, blue, indigo, and violet—blended together. You can see these colors in the form of a rainbow or **spectrum** if you pass a beam of light through an angled piece of glass, called a **prism**. Visible light is just a small part of a much larger spectrum of energy called the **electromagnetic spectrum**. Visible light is located in the middle of the electromagnetic spectrum and is the only part that can be seen by the human eye.

At one end of the electromagnetic spectrum, the waves are long. At the other end of the spectrum, the waves are short. The

Two beams of white light are passed through prisms to form two separate spectra. Notice the additional color effects where the spectra intersect.

What Is Visible?

"Visible light" is a relative term. We normally define it according to what humans can see, but it has different limits for other creatures on our planet. Bees, for example, can see in ultraviolet light. For a bee gathering nectar and pollen, flowers provide a spectacular show, with many colors and shades that our eyes miss entirely. Off the other end of the "visible" scale, some snakes find their prey by sensing infrared (heat) rays from warm animal bodies. Heat-sensitive pits on a rattlesnake's face can detect temperature differences of only thousandths of a degree. These heat sensors form a fuzzy infrared image of the prey so the snake can locate it even in the dark.

Scientists have copied the idea of seeing with heat sensors to develop night-vision goggles that allow people to see in the dark. In these devices, heat sensors detect small temperature differences in objects. The goggles translate that information into an image that humans can see. Infrared video cameras allow firefighters to move through smoke-filled buildings, using the display to find people who need to be rescued and to detect dangerous "hot spots" in the fire.

shorter the waves, the greater the energy they contain. The longest waves in the spectrum, which have the least amount of energy, are radio waves. The other radiations, in order along the spectrum, are microwaves, infrared radiation, visible light, ultraviolet radiation, X rays, and finally gamma rays, which have the shortest wavelengths and contain the greatest amount of energy.

Animal "Eyes"

Most animals have some sort of structure that can sense light. The simplest form of these organs is the **eyespot**. This is a clump of **pigment** (colored chemical) on the body surface that can detect light energy. The light-sensitive eyespot can tell the difference between light and dark, but it cannot make out any images. The single-celled euglena, for instance, has a red eyespot. This tiny freshwater creature is like an animal in some ways and like a plant in others. It can swim through the water and eat bits of matter, but it can also use sunlight to make food by photosynthesis, the way plants do. The euglena's eyespot gives it the information it needs to swim toward the sunlit areas bright enough for it to make its own food.

A number of **invertebrates** (animals without backbones), including flatworms and starfish, also have eyespots. The ability to detect light

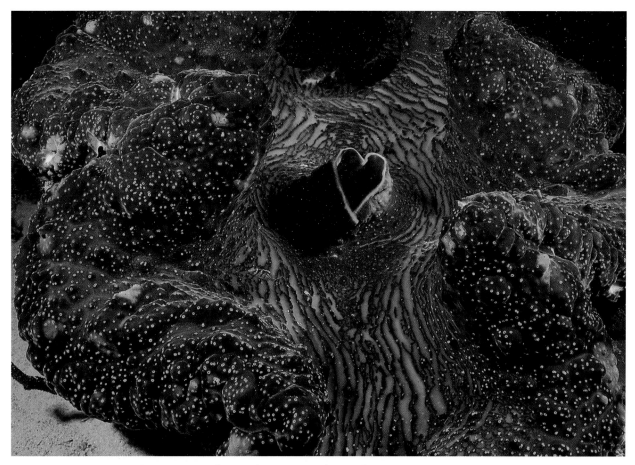

Invertebrates, such as the giant clam shown here, can see light with eyespots that are on the surface of the body.

allows the animals to move away from lighted areas to places where they may be less visible to predators.

The usefulness of an eyespot is very limited. It does not give an animal a picture of the world. Being able to *see* objects provides advantages in finding food and avoiding enemies. Eyes, the organs for seeing, have a much more complicated structure than a simple eyespot. Most **vertebrates** (animals with backbones), including humans, have a pair of eyes. Each one is shaped like a ball filled with fluid. Light rays enter the eye through an opening at the front, are **focused** (bent so that they form a clear image) by a transparent **lens**, and are detected by **photosensors**, a layer of light-sensitive cells at the back of the eyeball. Messages from these photosensors are then sent to the brain.

The basic design of the eye as an organ for seeing is so effective that two separate groups of animals independently developed the same design over the long course of **evolution**, the development of living organisms on our planet. Cats, dogs, mice, birds, lizards, and fish all have eyes that are basically similar to ours because we are relatively close relatives, all descended from common vertebrate ancestors. But squids and octopuses also have eyes with the same basic design, even though they are invertebrates whose ancestors took a very different path of evolution.

One group of invertebrates, the arthropods (crustaceans, spiders, and insects), developed a rather different kind of eye: **compound eyes**. Most of these creatures have both "simple eyes" and compound eyes. Each "simple eye" of an arthropod contains only a single lens and cannot focus well. Compound eyes, however, are made up of dozens, hundreds, or even thousands of tiny lenses. Each of these lenses focuses a picture of one tiny part of the animal's environment. The many tiny pictures fit together to form a single large picture, much as the many small colored tiles of a mosaic fit together to make a large picture.

The compound eye is very good for spotting moving objects. When something moves across an insect's **field of vision** (the area of its surroundings that it can see without turning its head), light rays reflected from it strike a series of lenses in its compound eye. The photosensors of each lens are activated in turn, alerting the insect to the movement and tracing its path.

How We See

Our eyes work somewhat like a camera. In a camera, a lens focuses rays of light onto the film, where light-sensitive chemicals react. The exposed area can then be developed by other chemicals to form an image or photograph of the scene that the camera "saw." The diaphragm controls the amount of light that enters the camera. For the clearest pictures in a bright room, the diaphragm opening is small and stays open for a short time. In dim light, the diaphragm is opened wider and stays open longer.

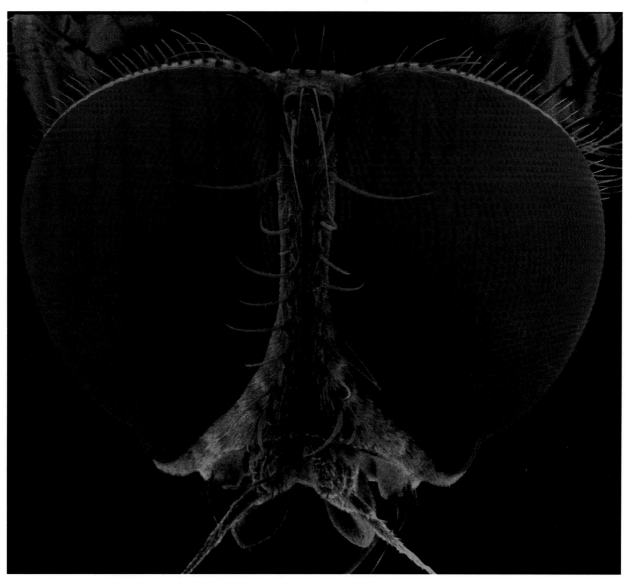

*This image of the head of a housefly
shows the thousands of tiny lenses that form compound eyes.*

In the human eye, light rays enter the eye through an opening
at the front, called the **pupil**. A round, muscular structure, the **iris**,
surrounds the opening and can make it larger or smaller to limit the
amount of light coming in (much like the diaphragm of a camera).
Behind the opening is the lens, which bends the light rays, changing

their direction as they pass into the eye. After passing through the fluid in the eyeball, the light rays are focused onto the **retina**, a layer of light-sensitive cells that line the back of the eyeball. Unlike camera film, whose light-sensitive chemicals can be used only once, the photosensors in the retina contain light-sensitive chemicals that are used over and over again.

Like the camera, the human eye has a focusing system that lets us see at varying distances. When focusing on an image, the lens of the eye must make adjustments so that light rays reflected from objects of interest will fall exactly on the retina. Muscles pull on the lens to make it flatter to view distant objects; they relax, allowing it to take a more curved shape, for looking at nearby objects. This change in the curvature of the lens is called **accommodation**.

Because of the way the light rays are bent, the image formed on the retina is upside down. This image is turned into nerve signals, which are then sent to the brain along the thick cord of nerve cells that form the **optic nerve**. Special areas of the brain are devoted to receiving and analyzing the messages from the eyes. The brain makes sense out of the information from the eyes and turns the image upright, producing the images that we see.

Machine Vision
Scientists have expanded our remarkable senses by developing machines with

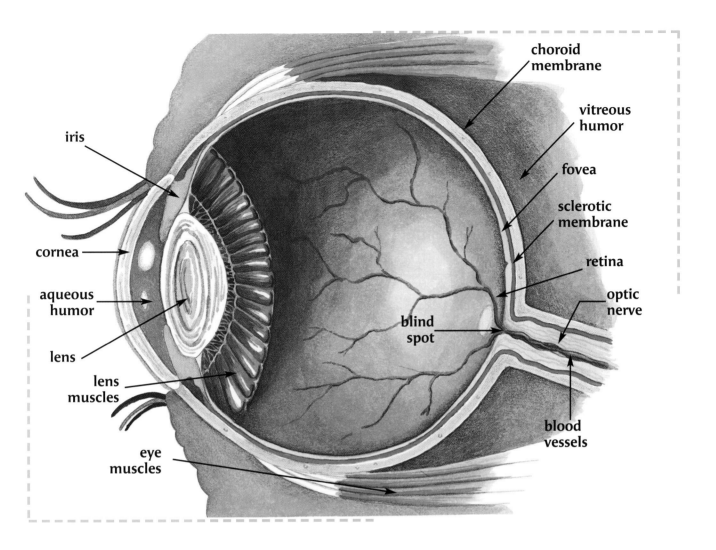

their own kind of "eyes." Like our vision, machine vision uses sensors to detect light energy. The **electric eye** is one kind of sensor that is used in a variety of common devices. Electric eyes are used to set off a burglar alarm, open doors, ring a buzzer, or turn lights on and off automatically.

How does an electric eye respond to light? When light hits this artificial sensor, the light energy is converted to an electric current. If the beam of light is broken by an object that enters its path, the electric current is interrupted, triggering a reaction. For instance, a burglar alarm may send out infrared rays across a room. If someone walks through these invisible rays, the break in the beam automatically sounds the alarm. Automatic door openers operate in a similar way. A detector placed near the door sends out a beam of light. When a person approaches the door, the beam is broken, and the door opens. The door will remain open until the person has passed through. Electric eyes are also used to turn streetlights and house lights on and off according to changes in light intensity. At twilight when the sky begins to darken, the lights turn on; at dawn, the lights turn off.

Machine vision allows assembly-line factories to use robots to improve production. Using a sensor, along with a video camera, a computer, and a few other components, automated machines are able to find and identify parts, as well as sort, count, measure, and verify objects. Machine vision is helpful in the production line because robots with "artificial eyes" can detect defects in less time than human inspectors.

three
Seeing colors

What would life be like if we could see the world only in black and white and shades of gray? We could not recognize colors: The grass and trees would not look green. The sky would not look blue. Flowers would not appear in shades of red, pink, yellow, orange, or purple.

Without colors, we would see the world rather like black-and-white movies. Could anybody live like that? Actually, scientists believe that animals such as dogs, cats, horses, and mice *do* live like that. These animals probably do not see the world in color. They do live in a sort of black-and-white movie.

Scientists have evidence that humans and monkeys are the only mammals able to see in color. Many fishes, insects, reptiles, and daytime birds also see in color, but they probably see somewhat different colors than humans do. Animals that cannot see in color still get plenty of visual information. Zebras, for instance, can see only various shades of gray, but they can quickly detect the movement of an approaching lion.

Inside the Photosensors

We know that the retina focuses the images that we see. But how does it make the images so clear, sharp, and colorful? And why do some creatures see in color while others do not?

The retina contains two kinds of photosensors: rods and cones. The **rod cells** are shaped like short, straight sticks. The cones are shaped somewhat like ice-cream cones. We need both rods and

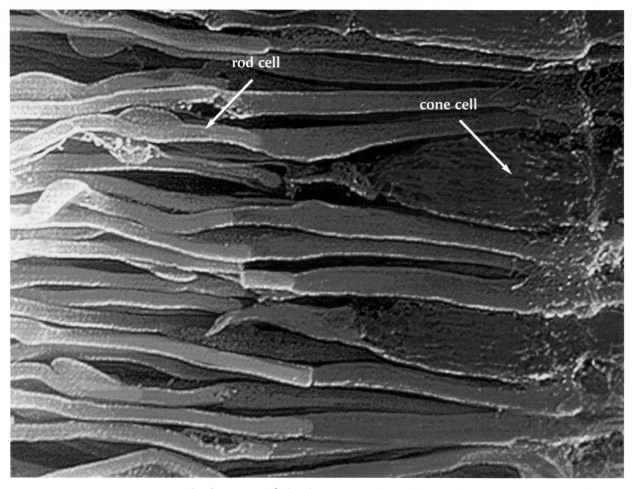

A close-up of the human retina shows that our eyes contain many more rod cells than cone cells. Rod cells help us see in dimly lit surroundings, while cone cells are responsible for our ability to see color.

cones for good vision. Our eyes contain many more rod cells than cone cells.

Rods are very sensitive. They are stimulated even by dim light, which gives us our night vision. (Bright light stimulates them so much that they are overloaded and turn off temporarily.) Although rods are very good at detecting motion, the vision they provide is blurry and unclear.

How do we see in dim light? Rods contain **rhodopsin**, a pigment that is also called visual purple. The more rhodopsin there is in the rods, the more sensitive our eyes are to the light. When light hits rhodopsin, it breaks down into two smaller parts, opsin and retinal. This chemical breakdown stimulates the optic nerve, and this allows us to see. Eventually, the opsin and retinal are chemically put back together, and rhodopsin is restored to the cells. In bright sunlight, all the rhodopsin in the rods is broken down. So if you walk into a darkened theater on a sunny afternoon, at first you can't see anything. But eventually the rhodopsin in the rods is rebuilt. Now even the dim lights in the theater are enough for you to find your seat and settle down to watch the movie.

Color My World

Have you ever noticed that in dim light you cannot see colors, only the shapes of objects? Objects appear in shades of gray in low-light conditions, because the rods cannot distinguish colors. **Cone cells**, which are sensitive only to bright light, are responsible for color vision. When you walk outside on a moonlit evening, your cone cells will not function; only the rod cells are stimulated.

All of the cone cells are located in the **fovea**, a small portion of the retina directly behind the lens. The image formed on the fovea is much clearer and more detailed than the image projected onto the rest of the retina, where there are only rods.

How can cone cells detect color? The human eye contains three kinds of cone cells, each containing a slightly different rhodopsin. Like the pigment in the rods, the rhodopsin in a cone cell is made up of retinal and opsin, but the opsins of the three kinds of cones differ slightly. Each opsin is stimulated when it absorbs light of a particular band of wavelengths. For instance, one kind of opsin is stimulated most by red light, another by green light, and the third by blue light. When cones of more than one kind are stimulated, the combined nerve signals are sent to the brain and interpreted as a particular color.

Combining the sense messages from different cones to produce a perceived color is like mixing two colors of paint to get another color. For instance, if you mix blue and red paint, you get purple. Similarly, when both red and blue cones are stimulated, you see purple. When using paints, you can blend the three **primary colors** (red, yellow, and blue) to produce dozens or even hundreds of color shades. Notice that the color set of your cones is slightly different—

DID YOU KNOW?

There are about 160,000 sensors per square millimeter in the fovea of a human eye; a hawk's fovea has about 1 million! That is why a hawk's vision is about eight times as sharp as ours— sharp enough to spot a mouse scurrying through the grass far below.

The Colors We See

Why is the sky blue? Why is the grass green? Why is my shirt red? The colors we see are the ones that are reflected, not absorbed. For instance, the sky is blue because the earth's atmosphere absorbs light of all the colors in the visible spectrum *except* the color blue, which is reflected. So the sky appears blue. A red shirt looks red because the dye in it reflects the red light that hits it, while the other colors of the spectrum are absorbed and disappear. Grass is green because the green pigment chlorophyll in its leaves absorbs most of the sunlight that strikes it but does not absorb green light, which is reflected back to our eyes. Plants use absorbed light energy to produce their own food. Green, which is so typical of plants, is actually the color of the only light they *don't* use.

red, green, and blue (RGB)—but blending them produces all the other colors.

On a computer screen, colors are also produced by combining different amounts of red, green, and blue. Programs for computer graphics allow the user to increase or decrease the RGB intensities to give a picture a very different look. Computer monitors can be set to display millions of different colors. This is far more than the 150 to 200 colors the average person can distinguish, but the many shadings of color help to give computer graphics and photos a richly detailed, lifelike appearance.

We can see how important both rods and cones are for good human vision. Some animals, however, do not have both rods and cones. Although their vision may not be as good as ours in some respects, it is usually well suited to the animal's behavior and environment. Nocturnal animals, such as ferrets and raccoons, have only rods in their retinas, and no color vision. The many rods allow them to see in the dark when they are most active. Diurnal animals, such as chipmunks and ground squirrels, have only cones in their retinas, so they can see sharp images during the day when they are most active. Birds that are active during the day, most reptiles, and fishes have good color vision, but frogs and salamanders are color-blind. Octopuses and squids, which developed their eyes along a separate path of evolution from the vertebrates, can see and distinguish colors quite well.

Some animals, such as turtles and birds, have as many as five kinds of cone cells (humans have only three), each of which contains a different pigment. These animals have better color vision than we do. Their extra cones probably allow them to distinguish more colors than we can.

Insects have very good color vision. Flowers pollinated by insects often have brightly colored flowers to attract their pollinators. When scientists learned to produce and use ultraviolet light, it

These images show the difference between what a flower looks like
to humans (left) and what a flower looks like to some insects (right) that can
distinguish different shades of ultraviolet light.

Are You Color-blind?

About 8 percent of human males, and about 0.5 percent of females, are unable to distinguish some or all of the colors most people see. Those with this hereditary condition are lacking one or more of the kinds of cones. About three-quarters are red-green color-blind—either the red or the green cones are missing, and they cannot distinguish between red and green. Blue weakness, due to a lack of blue cones, is much rarer. Rarest of all—less than one in a thousand—are the people who are *really* color-blind and have no color sensors. For them the world is like a black-and-white movie, with everything in black, white, and shades of gray.

These photographs show the difference between normal vision (left) and the vision of a person with red-green color-blindness (right). Notice how difficult it would be to distinguish the color of the red socks if you were color-blind.

was discovered that many flowers have ultraviolet color patterns, too. Although our eyes can't pick up ultraviolet colors, some insects have visual pigments that are stimulated by ultraviolet light. Researchers studying bees, for example, were able to train them to come to a feeding dish with sugar water, marked with particular colors, including some with ultraviolet wavelengths. The bees can distinguish various shades of ultraviolet just as we can tell the difference between, say, red and orange or blue and green.

Color Enhancing

A microscope or telescope can give us fascinating glimpses of things that are too small or too far to see with our own eyes. But the pictures these devices provide are usually in black and white, or there may not be much natural color variation in the objects they show us. It can be rather hard to make out details in a picture made up of shades of gray. After microscopes were invented, scientists studying tiny organisms or individual cells and tissues learned to improve the picture by using "stains"—special dyes that were taken up only by a particular kind of structure, making it stand out vividly from the rest of the picture. Such stains changed the things that were being viewed. With the development of computers, it became possible to selectively add color highlights to photographs without harming or changing the real objects.

Using **color enhancement**, researchers have been able to learn a lot more about the structures of very tiny objects. Some, such as viruses and the coiled chains of DNA (the chemicals of heredity) inside our own cells, are so small that they cannot be seen with an ordinary light microscope.

Color enhancement has also been used to bring out the details of pictures taken by telescopes and the cameras on space probes. Without the added color, pictures of the rings of Saturn, for example, and the surface of the Moon and Mars would be far less vivid. Color provides additional information and makes the photos more interesting and pleasant to look at.

The addition of color makes it possible to get more information out of weather photos taken by cameras on satellites. These cameras use film sensitive to infrared light, producing images in

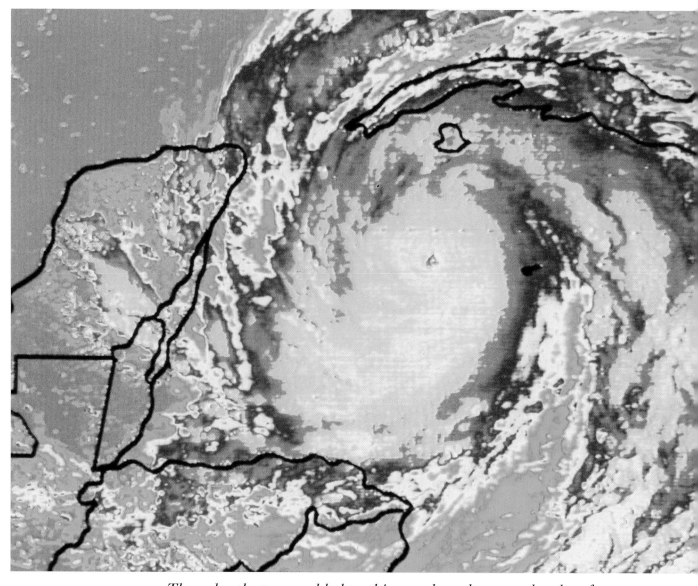

The color that was added to this weather photograph taken from a satellite in 1988 shows the intensity of hurricane Gilbert.

shades of gray that show small variations in temperature among cloud patterns. The highest cloud tops, which can bring on the strongest thunderstorms, are the coldest. Assigning a different color to each temperature makes it much easier to see which cloud formations are the highest.

four
The mind's eye

Every day, our eyes are constantly taking in information. In the morning you look at your face in the mirror while you brush your teeth and comb your hair. Would your spoon miss the cereal bowl if you tried to eat breakfast without looking? At school you have to look at the chalkboard, at textbooks, and at things you are writing or drawing. You use your eyes to recognize friends. In fact, you could even recognize people you know if you saw just the back of their heads or the way they walk. At home, watching TV, playing catch in the backyard, or surfing the Internet on a computer all involve looking and seeing.

Much of what we know about the world comes through our eyes. But alone, the eyes cannot make sense of the visual world. It would all be meaningless if it were not for the brain. Photoreceptors turn the light that enters the eyes into nerve signals. These messages are sent to the brain, where they are analyzed and interpreted into the images that we "see." So in a sense, we also see with our brains, not just with our eyes.

We aren't born with a brain able to interpret all the messages from the sense receptors. Our brain learns with each new experience. When the brain is presented with something unfamiliar, it searches for familiar patterns from past experiences. The brain is always taking in information and trying to make sense of it so we can stay connected to the world.

DID YOU KNOW?

A sharp blow to the head can make you "see stars," or bright flashes of light, because the back of the brain bangs against the bony skull. The impact stimulates neurons of the visual center, just as though they had received strong nerve messages from the photosensors in the retina.

Learning to See

What if we came into a world without any light or visual images? In a variety of experiments, researchers have shown how our brain needs to learn from visual experiences before it can interpret what it "sees." In one experiment, for instance, a newborn kitten was raised in the dark for the first few months of its life. Even though the kitten's eyes and brain seemed to be normal, it remained blind. This happened because the kitten lacked visual stimuli during a critical time in its early development. Similarly, a kitten that had one eye closed for the first few months lost vision in that eye but could see well through the open one. When another kitten was raised in an environment where it could see only horizontal lines, it had trouble perceiving objects with vertical patterns.

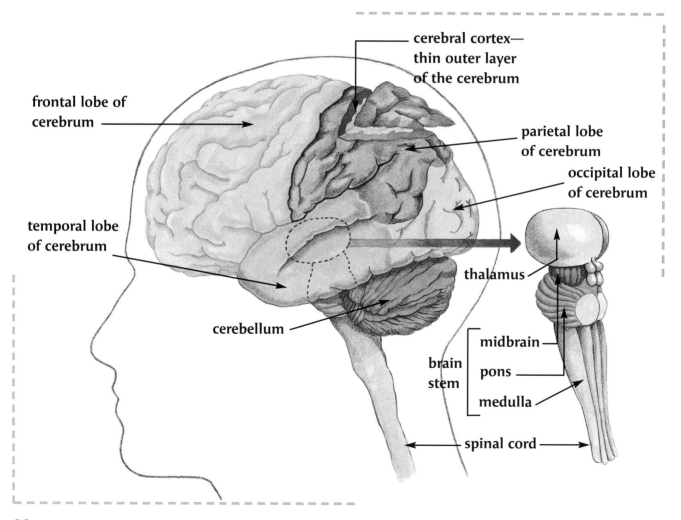

frontal lobe of cerebrum

cerebral cortex— thin outer layer of the cerebrum

parietal lobe of cerebrum

occipital lobe of cerebrum

temporal lobe of cerebrum

thalamus

cerebellum

brain stem

midbrain

pons

medulla

spinal cord

The brain is constantly trying to make sense of the world. It makes amazing adjustments in interpreting the messages sent by the eyes. It can correct distortions of images and fill in missing parts. For instance, in experiments at Innsbruck University in Austria, researchers tried wearing distorting glasses that made images seem blurred, with straight lines curved and the angles all out of proportion. They wore these glasses all the time. After a week or so, the distortions seemed to fade away and everything looked normal again. Then, when they took the glasses off, the world seemed distorted once more, and it was some days before their brains relearned to see things properly.

How the Brain Sees

Everything about us—our memories, thoughts, plans, attitudes, and personality—are all stored in the brain. The largest part of the brain, with which we think, remember, make decisions, and control the movements of the body, is called the **cerebrum**. Actually, most of this activity takes place in the **cerebral cortex**, the thin, outermost layer of the brain. This layer, less than 0.25 inch (6 millimeters) thick, contains billions of **neurons** (nerve cells) that receive messages from sense receptors and send out messages to control the activities of the body.

The cerebrum is separated into two halves, or **hemispheres**: the left and the right. The two hemispheres are not completely separated; deep inside the brain, a thick cable of nerve fibers called the **corpus callosum** links the two halves together. Strangely, most of the nerves connecting the cerebrum to the rest of the body cross over to the opposite side as they enter the brain. The brain's crisscross wiring means that movements on the left side of the body are controlled by the right side of the brain, and vice versa, and most of the sense messages

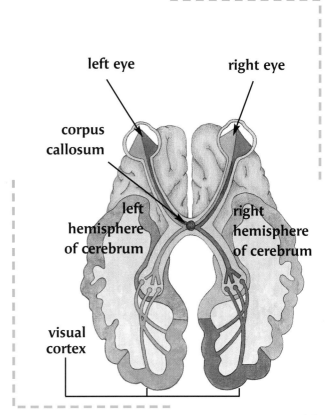

What a Split Brain Sees

Surgeons have treated some patients with severe epilepsy (a disease that produces seizures) by cutting their corpus callosum. This causes a condition called split brain, in which there is no communication between the two hemispheres. In experiments, split-brain volunteers were shown a series of pictures made up of two half-pictures joined in the middle. One picture, for example, might show half the face of a child on the left side and half the face of an old man on the right. The volunteer does not realize there is anything unusual about such pictures. If asked what the picture shows, she answers, "An old man." That is what her left brain saw and passed on the information to the speech center, which is usually in the left hemisphere. But if asked to point with her left hand to the picture she saw among a group of complete pictures spread out on the table, she points to the picture of the child. That is what her right brain saw and communicated to the part of the right hemisphere controlling the movements of her left hand.

that reach either hemisphere come from the opposite side of the body. The nerve connections from the eyes are a special case. Messages from the photoreceptors in each retina that correspond to the left half of the visual field go to the right side of the brain, while those from the right side of the visual field are sent to the left side of the brain. So for each eye, some of the nerve connections are crisscross, while others go straight to the hemisphere on the same side.

Researchers have found that particular areas of the cerebral cortex are associated with specific functions. The part that controls vision is called the **visual cortex**, or vision center. It is located in the back of the brain, in the region of each hemisphere called the **occipital lobe**. If you put your hand on the back of your head, you are touching the part of your skull that covers the visual cortex. All the messages from the retinas are sent to the visual cortex for processing.

Artificial Eyes

Imagine that you have a serious eye disorder that impairs your vision significantly. The thought of losing your sight is frightening. But scientists have been working hard on artificial eyes that can help people with impaired vision. The best progress so far has been made in projects focusing on people with macular degeneration and retinitis pigmentosa. In these eye disorders the retina is damaged, but the nerve cell pathways to the brain remain unharmed.

Artificial vision systems now under development use special glasses equipped with a tiny camera that converts images of the visual field to pulses of laser or infrared light. A transmitter sends the light pulses to tiny computer-like microchips on the inner surface of the retinas, which convert the visual information in the laser pulses to electrical signals. Implanted electrodes stimulate nerve cells that send messages to the brain.

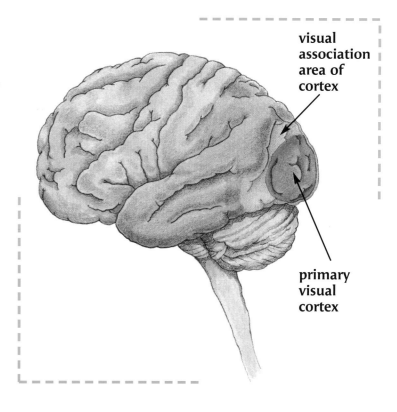

visual association area of cortex

primary visual cortex

One version of the artificial eye, now being developed by researchers at the University of Michigan and the University of Texas in Austin, uses tiny lenses less than a millimeter in diameter and laser transmitters small enough to fit on a microchip. This artificial eye will be able to detect not only visible but also ultraviolet and infrared light. Thus it could be used for both day and night vision and could also be incorporated into navigation systems of vehicles and robots.

Another approach to artificial vision systems, being developed at the University of Utah, sends video signals from a camera mounted in a pair of glasses to electrodes implanted in the visual cortex, where they stimulate individual nerve cells.

Robot Vision

How would you like to have a robot pet? In 1999, Sony began selling a highly sophisticated robot dog. AIBO (named for the Japanese word for "pal" and also an abbreviation for *a*rtificial *i*ntelligence ro*bo*t) looks and acts very much like the real thing. AIBO has sensors very similar to a person's, which allows it to perceive its environment and communicate with people. AIBO contains a special color camera and can search for its favorite colors. The camera and an infrared distance sensor work together

AIBO, the advanced robot dog by Sony, is able to express emotions through sounds and motions, and even wags its tail when it's happy. Early in 2001, Sony introduced a 2nd Generation AIBO that has a greater ability to express emotion for a more intimate connection with people.

to detect obstacles and keep AIBO from bumping into things, but black objects, which absorb infrared rays, are hard for it to see. It also has some trouble seeing the floor under low-light conditions. AIBO is programmed to learn from experiences and the environment, the way a child would go through developmental stages.

Developing vision systems for a robot that can move around on its own in the real world is a very complicated task. A detailed perception of the environment must be carefully coordinated with the robot's own movements and responses—the way our brains coordinate the input from our eyes with our movements in the world around us. The machines in automated factories that do various manufacturing tasks usually work with a limited assortment of objects, which have regular shapes and predictable positions. "Robots" that do more demanding things, such as brain surgery, are usually guided to some degree by human operators. So far, the idea of household robots that can dust, vacuum, wash dishes, and mow the lawn is still a dream for the future.

five
Seeing shapes

Have you ever looked through someone else's glasses? Things probably looked pretty blurry to you and really out of focus. To the person who wears these glasses, however, everything looks clear.

The natural lens of the eye bends light rays so that the light from each point on an object falls exactly on a single point on the inner surface of the retina, producing an image of the object's shape. The muscles around the lens can change its shape to bring near or distant objects into a clear focus. But some people have lenses that aren't shaped quite perfectly and cannot focus clearly on some objects. A person who cannot see close objects clearly but can see distant objects is farsighted. Someone who cannot see distant objects clearly but can see close objects is nearsighted. Some people who have normal vision become farsighted as they get older because the focusing muscles get weaker.

Using glass or plastic lenses in front of the eyes can help to focus the light rays for people whose own lenses cannot do the job well enough. Glasses or contact lenses are carefully fitted according to the person's focusing needs. That is why looking through another person's glasses probably would not produce a clear picture on your retina.

Shaping Up
If you look at a black-and-white photograph through a magnifying glass, you will find that the picture is made up of hundreds or thousands of tiny dots. Some are darker than others. They range from

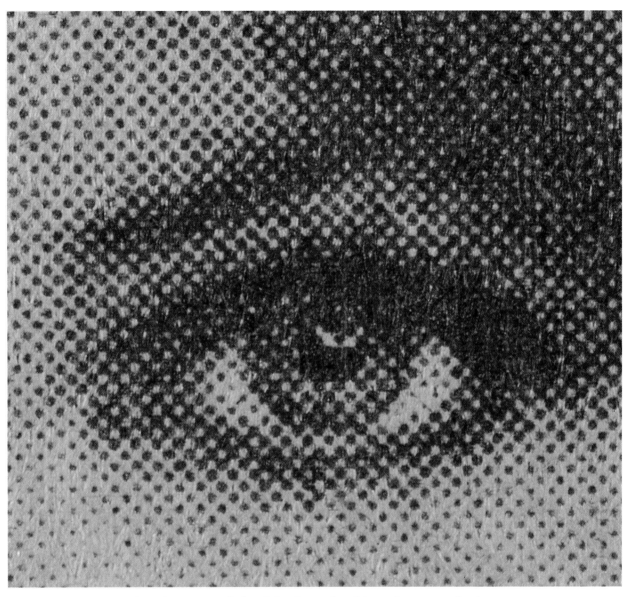

*The close-up of this black-and-white photograph shows
that it is made up of thousands of tiny dots in various shades of gray. Computer
programs can change the darkest dots to black and the lighter dots to white, which
produces a black-and-white line drawing.*

black through many different shades of gray to pure white. Your vision blends the various shades into a smooth image that shows rounded contours and sharp edges.

Actually, you have a similar image forming on your retina as you look at the picture. Thousands of neurons connected to the retina are sending signals to your brain. Each of these signals corresponds to a group of photosensors on the retina. It contains information on the intensity of the light falling on the photosensors. Some of the nerve cells in the visual cortex that analyze the incoming information are particularly sensitive to contrasts between light and dark. Together they build up a picture that shows the darkness of the shades, as well as the sharp edges, the smooth contours, and the texture of the image.

Computer programs have been developed to analyze the information in an image in much the same way the brain does. By emphasizing contrasts, these programs can transform a black-and-white photo into a line drawing. The original image is formed by thousands of dots of various shades of gray. The computer changes all the darkest dots in the original image to black dots and the lighter ones to white dots. This shows the contrasts in the image more clearly and reveals the edges of all the objects in it. The result is a black-and-white line drawing.

What's on TV?

The picture on a TV or computer screen is made up of tiny dots called **pixels** (short for "picture element"). These pixels, which may number about a million or more, are arranged on a rectangular grid, much like the stitches in needlepoint. For a black-and-white picture, each pixel is given a number that indicates its brightness. For a color picture, each pixel is given three numbers that represent the brightness of each of the primary colors, red, green, and blue. A graphics card is used to turn the arrangement of dots into signals. The lighted red, green, and blue dots combine to form a full-color picture.

The dots in a black-and-white or color picture are drawn on the screen one line at a time, but this happens so fast that we can't see the process—we just see the whole picture. A standard television picture is built up from 480 horizontal lines of pixels. In HDTV

Here, you can see the tremendous difference between the clarity of a teddy bear on a standard television screen (top) and an HDTV screen (bottom).

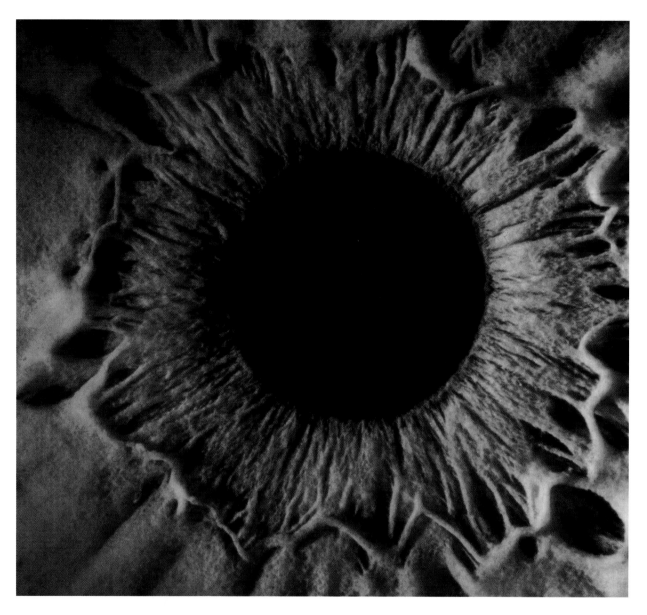

This close-up shows the pattern of the markings in a person's iris. Iris-recognition technology can be used for security purposes to identify a person by these patterns.

(high definition TV), the picture has up to 1,080 lines, making it as clear and sharp as the picture on the screen in a movie theater.

Tricking the Seeing Brain

The brain is so used to finding patterns that it looks for patterns whether they are there or not. For example, ancient people looked up at the sky filled with stars and linked various groups of them together mentally to form the outlines of people, animals, and objects, such as the Big Dipper. The brain fills in any missing pieces of information to complete the pictures. This tendency is what "tricks" us when we see optical illusions. Optical illusions occur because of the way the brain analyzes the information from the eyes, not because of what the eyes actually see.

Positive ID

It takes just a split second to recognize a familiar face. How do you do it? Your brain notes the important features, such as the eyes, nose, mouth, general shape of the face, and hair, and compares them to the "database" of faces stored in your memory. (Researchers have found that a special part of the brain is involved in recognizing and remembering faces, separate from other kinds of memory.)

Find Your Blind Spot

One of the most amazing optical illusions is something you experience all the time but never even realize it. There is a spot on each retina where all the nerves carrying messages from the photosensors come together as they form the optic nerve leading into the brain. Within this small oval area, about 2 millimeters (less than a tenth of an inch) wide, there are no rods or cones. Any light rays that fall upon it are invisible to you, because you have no photosensors there. But you do not realize you have a "blind spot" in each eye because your brain fills in the missing part of the picture.

To demonstrate this, all you need is a cotton Q-tip. Close your left eye and stare at a small object or spot across the room. Holding the Q-tip out at arm's length, line it up so that the tip of the cotton exactly covers the spot. While still staring at the same spot, slowly move the Q-tip to the right until the cotton disappears. This is your blind spot. You no longer see the white cotton. Instead you seem to see an unbroken background scene. Now raise your arm slightly so that the middle of the stick is in the blind spot. You won't see any gap in the stick. This time, your brain supplies an image of the rest of the stick, filling in the missing details.

We develop the ability to recognize faces very early. Infants quickly learn to recognize the faces of their parents or other people who care for them. We can even recognize the face of a person we used to know, in spite of the changes the years have made.

Computer scientists have developed programs for recognizing faces. The features are analyzed to form a grid of visual information, which is then compared to the set of faces in the computer's database. Although people's faces may have distinctive features, some people resemble others. Just as eyewitnesses may incorrectly identify a suspect in a police lineup, ID programs based on the whole face may also be misled by similarities of one face to another. But people do have some features that are unique. Fingerprints have long been used for identification: No two people (except, perhaps, for identical twins) have exactly the same patterns of lines, loops, and whorls on the skin of their fingertips. Researchers have found that the patterns of the blood vessels and other details of the retina are also distinctive. The markings of the iris (the colored portion of the eye) are unique for each person, as well. As more powerful computers have become readily available, new techniques for foolproof identification have been developed on the basis of computer imaging.

Has your mom or dad ever tried to withdraw money from the ATM machine, and then realized they forgot the PIN number? No PIN number, no money. But in Swindon, England, people who forget their PIN numbers can access their accounts anyway. In a pilot test study, participating banks in Swindon are using iris-recognition technology, which identifies customers by patterns in the iris. This form of positive identification is an example of **biometrics**, a technology that can identify users by physical attributes such as face recognition, iris, retina, fingerprint, hand shape, or voice. These patterns are captured on camera and checked against recorded images in a database to verify a match. Iris and retinal biometric systems are the most reliable.

Biometrics sounds like it belongs in science fiction, but it is now making its way into the real world of business and government, as well as the lives of consumers and citizens. Biometrics is gradually becoming more and more accepted, due to our society's growing concern about security. We gain access to secured places or materials in two main ways: by using something a person knows (lock combination, PIN, or password) or with something a person has (ATM card, keys to file cabinets). In biometrics, people can gain access on the basis of who they are—their characteristics. This is something that cannot be lost, borrowed, or stolen.

What would it be like to have biometrics as an integral part of our society? Airports might be able to prevent terrorist attacks; banks and stores might be able to prevent criminal activity. Biometric technology is capable of tightening up security measures, but it also raises some concerns about individual privacy. Your movements can be tracked easily by these devices.

six
Seeing motion

Sports games usually involve a lot of concentration and a lot of action. A baseball batter watches the pitcher as he winds up his arm and throws the ball in the batter's direction. The ball comes at an amazing speed; it curves, then straightens out, and the batter watches carefully as he swings just in time to smack the ball over the right-field bleachers. What would a ball game be without motion? No swinging bats, no flying balls, no running players.

The eye is a powerful organ for sensing movement. Being able to see movement is essential for the survival of most animals, including humans. An animal needs to detect movement in order to hunt and escape predators. Like animals, early humans needed to hunt for food and stay safe from danger. Even today, we need to see motion so we can connect with the outside world. We use motion to communicate with others, moving our arms, our legs, and our facial expressions. We use motion detection to watch out for moving cars, buses, and trucks when we cross the street or ride a bike. Can you imagine life without the ability to see motion?

Scientists have been trying to learn more about motion detection by studying the motion detector experts of the animal world—frogs. Frogs are famous for their ability to spot a moving insect and zap it in an instant. Compared with those of humans, a frog's eyes are much simpler, which makes them easier to study. In fact, frogs have proved to be a very useful model in studying sight, especially that involving motion.

How a Frog Sees Motion

The frog's eyes give a much simpler view of the world than our eyes, but this is enough for its needs. To survive, a frog has to be able to catch its food and to keep from being caught by swooping birds or pouncing animals. A frog eats insects, which it catches with lightning flicks of its long tongue. Therefore the only details that are really important to a frog are moving things: small, insect-shaped objects moving toward it, which it can catch; large, threatening objects moving toward it, which may attack it; including shadows overhead, which may indicate the approach of a bird. With these three types of information available, a frog can react quickly. If an

This frog's eyes respond only to moving objects,
such as a threat or something to eat.

Electronic Frog Eyes

Since a frog's eye is designed to detect moving objects, researchers have used the frog as a model for creating electronic motion detectors. These electronic applications have been used to keep track of airplanes circling above an airport and thus feed information to computer-run air traffic-control systems. They can also be used in warning and defense systems that provide protection from attack by enemy missiles.

Imagine these electronic frog eyes being used to run an automatically guided automobile—a car operating without a human driver. In some ways, a driver is like a frog sitting on a lily pad. The driver must have a constant flow of information about approaching objects—cars, signposts, pedestrians crossing the road. But there are many other distracting details that are not important—cars on the other side of the road, billboards. All these details might cause a human driver to divert attention away from driving, but an automatic steering system with froglike electronic eyes would not notice them at all.

Such futuristic cars may not be too far off. In 1999, General Motors started a five-year government-sponsored project aimed at building a "smart car" that can avoid rear-end collisions. Equipped with radar to detect the movements of other vehicles, it will also have a camera to "see" the road ahead so that the car's computer brain can figure out which cars are in the same lane, even if the road is curving.

insect is flying toward it, the frog can follow the insect's flight with its motion-sensitive eyes and catch it when it comes within range of the darting tongue. If a threat is looming near, the frog jumps—hopefully into the water, but if it lands on the ground, it can always jump again. A frog has no need to be able to see a clear view of blades of grass or trees or rocks, or anything else that does not move; these details are usually not important in its world.

A frog sees motion when an object moves across the retina. When this happens, photosensors in the retina immediately send out messages that are relayed by the brain to the muscles. Most of the image processing is actually done in the retina, before any information reaches the frog's brain.

Scientists have discovered that a frog's retina contains five different kinds of cells, each contributing its own type of information, which together make up the frog's picture of the world. "Edge detectors" pick up the outlines of objects, provided that they are moving and have a shape that might prove "interesting." For example, in one experiment, the frogs did not respond to a motionless circle or square, nor to a moving square, but a rapid fire of messages traveled along the optic nerve whenever a circle was in motion. (A moving circle looks more like an insect than a square does.) The second group of cells, the "bug detectors," work to sharpen the outline and pinpoint the exact location of the moving object. "Event detectors" pick up the sensation of movement, and "dimming detectors" signal a sudden darkening that might mean a threatening shadow. Finally, the frog's eyes contain "color detectors," which are sensitive to only one color—a watery blue. These sense cells help the frog to jump toward the water, where it would have the best chance to escape from danger.

How We See Motion

Detecting movement is a bit more complicated for humans than it is for frogs. When a frog sees movement, the eye itself processes much of the incoming information, triggering an automatic response. But in humans, the eyes merely receive the incoming visual information and send it to the brain, where it is analyzed and processed. Scientists have found that there are special cells in an area of the visual cortex whose function is to detect movement.

When an image moves across our retinas, we see motion. Our peripheral

Motion Blindness

Can you imagine what life would be like if you could not see motion? You would suddenly see someone right in front of you, but never saw the person move toward you. You might accidentally knock a glass off the table, but not see it fall. Suddenly it would appear as broken pieces on the floor. If you poured juice into a cup, you could see the cup's shape, color, and position on the table, but not the flow of liquid from the juice container to the cup. It would look frozen, like a waterfall turned to ice. So the cup would fill up with juice and spill over the sides. We normally do not realize just how important the ability to see motion is in our lives.

People with a rare condition called motion blindness do not see any motion or may not be able to perform certain motion-related tasks. Motion blindness occurs when there is damage to the pathway of nerve connections that lead to the area of the brain that analyzes motion. Motion blindness may develop after carbon monoxide poisoning, trauma, stroke, or degenerative diseases such as glaucoma, multiple sclerosis, or Parkinson's disease.

Is the farthest pool ball actually much smaller than the closest? Of course not. Our brain allows us to interpret that the ball is just moving away from us, not getting smaller.

vision is especially sensitive. We often spot things that move in the "corner of our eye." We can keep the moving object in our visual field when we move our eyeballs to follow it. This is called *tracking*. It is often necessary to turn the head or body to track a moving object. Imagine watching a tennis match without moving your head to watch the ball go from one side of the net to the other. It would be impossible to get the full picture without turning your head to keep the image in the visual field.

Our perception of motion is also affected by certain changes in the image, such as changes in focusing, size, and brightness. For instance, when an image appears to be getting smaller, your brain interprets it as an object that is moving away from you. Conversely, an image that appears to be getting larger is interpreted as an object that is moving toward you. You probably do not even realize that your brain is constantly making adjustments so you can make sense of the motion you are seeing. Your brain lets you know that your friends did not get bigger as they walked down the long school hallway to talk to you. They were merely moving toward you.

Motion Sickness

We can usually tell if something is moving or not. If you fly a paper airplane through the air, you can see that it is moving. When we look at cars or buses, we can see they are moving. But sometimes, objects look like they are moving when they are really motionless. For instance, when you sit in the backseat of a moving car and look outside, what do you see? The trees, houses, and parked cars are all whizzing by your window. They look like they are moving, but in reality, they are not. This can cause a problem in your perception of motion. Your eyes see movement, but your body doesn't feel any movement. These mixed messages may result in motion sickness. Your stomach feels queasy, your head hurts, and you may even vomit. Motion sickness can occur in cars, boats, trains, airplanes, and amusement park rides. Motion sickness is usually not a serious problem, but it can sure make you feel miserable.

The Illusion of Movement

When we watch a movie or TV, it seems as though we are seeing things moving—cars speed along the highway, ballplayers slide into a base or leap to catch a long fly ball. Actually, the images we see as "moving pictures" in movies are really sequences of still images

This sequence of still images shows the positions of a basketball player that can produce the illusion of movement if shown in quick succession.

on a strip of film. The images are displayed in such quick succession that our brains do not notice the black spots between each image; our minds blend the images to give the impression of a continuous scene in which things move. Scientists have found that images can be blended in this way when they are shown at a rate of about 50 per second. If the film moves more slowly than that, the picture tends to flicker. (Early movies were called "flicks" because of this effect.)

In television, each image in the sequence is drawn on the screen, line by line, too fast for us to perceive the individual stages of the process and fast enough to give the illusion of movement. Animations on a computer screen work the same way, showing a series of drawings.

seven
Seeing in 3-D

Close one eye and try to walk around the room. Was it difficult? Did you bump into anything? Walking around with one eye closed is not impossible, but it's much easier if you have both your eyes open. That is because seeing through just one eye gives you only part of the picture. The image looks flat and two-dimensional. This kind of vision, called **monocular vision**, makes it hard to judge depth and distance. But in **binocular vision** (viewing through two eyes), each eye sees an image at a slightly different angle. When you look at something with both eyes, the brain blends the two different images into a three-dimensional **stereoscopic** view. You can avoid bumping into a chair or other obstacles because you can tell if they are close to you or far away.

Two-Eyed View

Look at an object, such as a lamp, with your left eye closed. Open that eye and look at the lamp again, but with your right eye closed. Does it look as though the lamp moved? It didn't really move; you got that impression because each eye sees a different view of the scene. Although the visual fields of the two eyes are slightly different, there is a large area of overlap. The blending of the two images in the visual cortex produces an impression of distance and depth.

Humans depend on binocular vision to guide them through their lives, but it is not essential. Even with monocular vision, the brain picks up on visual cues to fill in the missing pieces. For

There is a limit to convergence. If we try to focus on something too close, we become "cross-eyed" and see a double image.

instance, if you see a man apparently next to a house that is much smaller than he is, you will automatically figure out that the house is considerably farther away than the man. An object that is partly blocking something else in the scene is interpreted as being closer—in front of the other object. Highlights and shadows help to give an impression of depth to an image. We can also judge distances through accommodation: As the shape of the lens is changed to focus on a nearby object, distant objects will appear blurry. In addition, the brain receives messages from the eye muscles that tell it when we are moving our eyes closer together to focus on a nearby object. (This adjustment is called **convergence**.) The eyes look straight ahead in parallel when gazing at things at a distance of about 20 feet (6 meters) or more.

In the animal world, birds and mammals that are predators depend on their binocular vision for survival. Like humans, predators have two eyes on the front of their head. Their forward-facing eyes can focus on the same object at the same time. They can get good depth perception and judge the size and distance of an object more accurately. This is essential for a cat about to pounce on a mouse or an owl swooping down. Good depth perception is also vital for a monkey leaping from branch to branch.

Typical prey animals such as rabbits and mice, on the other hand, depend on their monocular vision for survival. These animals have widely spaced eyes that are placed one on each side of the head. Their visual fields have very little overlap, which gives them no depth perception. However, the animal is able to see virtually 360 degrees without turning its head. It can spot a predator coming toward it from any direction, or focus on the food it is eating with one eye while watching for danger with the other.

Three-Dimensional Pictures

Look at a photograph. You can see the color and outlines of the people and the objects in it. But the images in the picture appear flat and two-dimensional, with no impression of depth. The images we see in photographs, TV, movies, and computers do not give a realistic view of the three-dimensional world we live in.

For over a century, people have been trying to turn two-dimensional pictures into three-dimensional images. In 1838, Sir Charles Wheatstone invented a primitive device called the stereoscope, which used a system of mirrors to view a series of pairs of drawings to produce a three-dimensional 3-D effect. This early device was rather bulky and complicated. Over the years, this technique was developed into much smaller and simpler viewing devices. In 1939 the Viewmaster was created as a home-entertainment device for both children and adults. People could see vivid three-dimensional images when they looked through the Viewmaster at a reel of stereo slides. Today the Viewmaster is marketed as a toy for children, but adults still enjoy it.

Most movies show ordinary two-dimensional images, but since the early 1950s some special features have been made in 3-D. The images appear so real that you almost feel as if you can touch them, and moving objects seem to leap out of the screen toward you. But you have to wear special glasses to see the 3-D effect. The lenses of the 3-D glasses are made of colored plastic film; one is red and the other is blue. Like the pictures in a stereoscope, each frame of the movie is composed of two images that partly overlap each other to produce depth. The colors of the two images are slightly different. The red lens in the special glasses filters out the red color in one image, making all the red details seem to disappear, while blues are turned into black. The blue lens cancels out the blue tones in the other image. So your two eyes see two slightly different images,

We can look to the side by moving our eyes in their sockets or turning our heads. Owls' eyes are pointed straight forward. An owl can't turn its eyes sideways, but it can turn its head so far that it is looking almost straight backward. It does this so quickly that it looks as though the owl's head is spinning around.

each missing one key color. Your brain puts these two images together to form a single 3-D picture.

A dramatic new way to make 3-D pictures, called **holography**, was invented in 1947 by the British physicist Dennis Gabor, who won a Nobel Prize for his idea. The first images using this technique (**holograms**) were not made until 1960.

A hologram is not only three-dimensional, it can be so complete that the viewer can look at it from different angles and even walk around and look at the back of the image. The hologram contains information about the size, shape, brightness, and contrast of the object. Holograms may show motion, change color, or even display different images when viewed at different angles; some seem to project an image out into the space in front of the picture.

Today holograms are commonly placed on credit cards, product labels, and decorative stickers. Holography is used in art and is also very useful in modern technology, for visualizing new designs and testing manufactured parts for defects. The displays on the control panels in airplanes and some high-tech cars are holograms. In the future, TV pictures may be transmitted as holograms, and the technique could also be used to store information in computers. Using holographic data storage, all the books in the Library of Congress could be stored in a block the size of a sugar cube!

Living in the Virtual World

Imagine climbing up Mount Everest, dancing in a music video, or meeting one of your favorite movie stars. These things sound like the kind of dreams you may have at night. But dreams like these can become a "reality"—at least, a virtual reality.

Virtual reality (or VR) is a simulation of an environment, created with computer hardware and software, and presented to the user so that it looks and feels like the "real thing." A person who wants to go on a virtual reality adventure must wear special goggles and gloves, which are hooked up to a computer. The glasses transmit a full-color image to each eye through a lens-and-mirror system. The image appears real, lifelike, and three-dimensional. The computer can create any kind of setting. A 3-D kitchen can be created from scratch with realistic floors, furnishings, colors, and

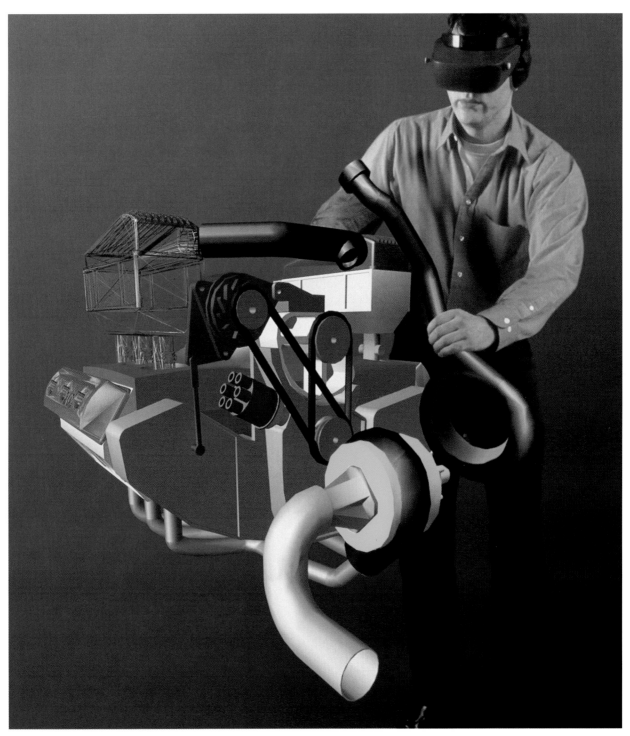

This engineer is saving costs and time by training on a virtual reality Porsche engine. The headset provides images and sounds of the engine and can present computer-generated responses to his actions by monitoring the engineer's movements.

textures. You can interact with people and objects that aren't really there.

Virtual reality is not just used for entertainment. In the automobile industry, for instance, cars are designed through virtual modeling using computer-produced holograms. The new designs can be put through tests on the computer to show how the car will behave under real road conditions, and how well it would survive a crash. This is much cheaper and faster than building actual models. VR is also being used in medical training. New doctors can practice surgical techniques on virtual patients with programmed coaching. If the doctors make mistakes, they don't risk the lives of any real patients.

eight
Seeing the invisible

Humans and many animals use light rays, detected by photosensors and analyzed by the visual area of the brain, to provide a clear and detailed picture of the world. But this is not the only way to "see." Bats have eyes, but they get their most detailed view of the world by interpreting the way sound waves bounce off objects. Whales and dolphins use the same sort of sonar to "see" things in the ocean. Some fishes that live in muddy streams find their prey and navigate by producing weak electric currents and analyzing the changes that objects produce in the patterns of the currents. Blind people get information about their surroundings through the use of other senses. They use touch to visualize the contours of people's faces or objects and to read words printed in Braille, with letters formed by patterns of raised dots. (This information is processed in the visual cortex.) Blind people may also learn to make small noises, such as clicks or finger snaps, and analyze the way they bounce off objects in much the same way as bats or dolphins.

People have built devices to use other forms of energy to "see" things that would not be visible to our eyes. The first microscopes used lenses to focus light rays to see very tiny things. Later, microscopes using X rays, beams of electrons, and sound waves were invented and made it possible to see even smaller things all the way down to single atoms. The first telescopes used light rays to see distant objects more clearly. Now we can also see the planets and distant stars with radiotelescopes that use radio waves to form the images. Artificial sensors and powerful computers are giving us a wealth of new information, constantly expanding our view of our world.

Glossary

accommodation—a change in the curvature of the lens that allows the eye to focus at varying distances.

binocular vision—viewing through two eyes, merging their slightly different and overlapping images to give a three-dimensional view.

biometrics—a technology that can identify users by physical attributes such as face recognition, iris, retina, fingerprint, hand shape, or voice.

cerebral cortex—the thin, outermost layer of the brain where most of its activity takes place.

cerebrum—the largest part of the brain, with which we think, remember, process sensory information, make decisions, and control the movements of the body.

color enhancement—a process that uses color to bring out fine details of pictures.

compound eyes—structures for vision that are made up of dozens, hundreds, or thousands of tiny lenses that focus a tiny part of the animal's environment. The many tiny pictures fit together to form a single large mosaic picture.

cone cells—light-sensitive cells that respond only to bright light and are responsible for color vision.

convergence—turning of the eyeballs inward, toward each other, to bring a nearby object into focus.

corpus callosum—a thick cable of nerve fibers deep inside the brain that links the two brain hemispheres and permits an exchange of information between them.

electric eye—a light-sensitive sensor that uses electricity to work devices such as door openers, buzzers, burglar alarms, and automatic lights.

electromagnetic spectrum—the whole range of energy, from radio waves to gamma rays.

evolution—the development of living organisms over a long period of time.

eyespot—a simple structure that certain animals use to sense light.

field of vision—the area of its surroundings that an animal can see without turning its head.

focusing—the bending of light rays to form a clear image.

fovea—a small portion of the retina directly behind the lens of the human eye, which contains all the cones and produces a clear, colorful image.

hemispheres—two halves of the brain, the left and the right.

holography—a technique for producing a complete, detailed, 3-D image of an object, using laser light. The image formed is called a *hologram*.

invertebrates—animals without backbones or an internal skeleton.

iris—a round muscular structure that surrounds the pupil. It controls the amount of light that enters the eye by making the pupil larger or smaller.

lens—the transparent structure in the eye that focuses light rays.

monocular vision—viewing through a single eye. Images appear flat and two-dimensional. This kind of vision makes it hard to judge depth and distance.

neurons—nerve cells.

occipital lobe—a region at the back of the brain that contains the vision center.

optic nerve—a thick cord of nerve cells that sends nerve signals from the eyes to the brain, where they are translated into meaningful images.

photosensors—light-sensitive structures that collect visual information.

pigment—a colored chemical.

pixels—picture elements; tiny dots arranged on a rectangular grid that produce the images on TV, movie, and computer screens.

primary colors—three colors: red, yellow, and blue, which can be blended to produce dozens or hundreds of shades of colors.

prism—an angled piece of glass that splits light into the spectrum of colors.

pupil—the opening at the front of the eyeball that allows light rays to enter.

reflection—the bouncing of light rays back toward their origin.

retina—a layer of light-sensitive cells that lines the back of the eyeball and receives the image formed by the lens.

rhodopsin—also called visual purple. Its chemical breakdown forms images on the retina that stimulate nerve cells connected to the brain.

rod cells—light-sensitive cells that are sensitive to dim light, providing night vision.

sensors—specialized structures that gather information about the world. They detect various types of energy and transmit signals to the brain.

spectrum—the band of colors produced by the separation of light of different wavelengths.

stereoscopic—pertaining to three-dimensional vision or producing the illusion of a 3-D image.

vertebrates—animals with a backbone and an internal skeleton.

virtual reality (VR)—a simulation of an environment, created with computer hardware and software and presented to the user (who may wear special goggles and gloves) so that it looks and feels like the "real thing."

visible light—the part of the electromagnetic spectrum that humans can see.

vision—sight; sensing with the eyes.

visual cortex—or vision center; the part of the brain that controls vision.

Further Reading

Barré, Michel. *Animal Senses*. Milwaukee, Wis.: Gareth Stevens Publishing, 1998.

Cobb, Vicki, *How to Really Fool Yourself: Illusions for All Your Senses*. New York: John Wiley & Sons, Inc., 1999.

Hellman, Hal. *Beyond Your Senses: The New World of Sensors*. New York: Lodestar Books, 1997.

Hickman, Pamela. *Animal Senses: How Animals See, Hear, Taste, Smell, and Feel*. Buffalo, N.Y.: Kids Can Press Ltd., 1998.

Llamas, Andreu. *The Five Senses of the Animal World: Sight*. New York: Chelsea House Publishers, 1995.

Parker, Steve. *Look at Your Body: Senses*. Brookfield, Conn.: Copper Beech Books, 1997.

Santa Fe Writers Group. *Bizarre & Beautiful Eyes*. Santa Fe, N.Mex.: John Muir Publications, 1993.

Tytla, Milan. *See Hear: Playing with Light and Sound*. Toronto, Ont.: Annick Press Ltd., 1994.

Internet Resources

charon.assert.ee/magic.htm
Welcome to the World of Magic.

cvs.anu.edu.au/andy/beye/beyehome.html
See the world through the eyes of a honey bee.

ibms50.scri.fsu.edu/~dennisl/CMS/activity/optical.html
Optical Illusions (includes some of the most common optical illusions).

nyelabs.kcts.org/teach/episodeguides/eg16.html
Bill Nye the Science Guy: Episode 16, Light and Color.

nyelabs.kcts.org/teach/episodeguides/eg20.html
Bill Nye the Science Guy: Episode 20, the Eyeball.

nyelabs.kcts.org/teach/episodeguides/eg27.html
Bill Nye the Science Guy: Episode 27, Light Optics.

www.aibo.com/ers_210/
AIBO homepage.

www.grand-illusions.com/gregory2.htm
"Introduction to Seeing," Richard Gregory.

www.grand-illusions.com/percept.htm
"Persistence of Vision," Stephen Herbert.

www.hhmi.org/senses
"Seeing, Hearing, and Smelling the World: New Findings Help Scientists Make Sense of Our Senses," The Howard Hughes Medical Institute.

www.holoworld.com
Holography Lasers and Holograms.

www.lhup.edu/~dsimanek/3d/illus2.htm
"Adding Depth to Illusions," Donald E. Simanek, December 1996.

www.magiceye.com/faq.htm
Magic Eye FAQ.

www.zdnet.com/anchordesk/story/story_3404.html
"5 Gee-Whiz Biometric Apps," Jesse Berst, May 1999.

www.zdnet.com/pcmag/stories/reviews/0,6755,392609,00.html
"Biometric Basics," Neil Randall, March 1999.

ww2010.atmos.uiuc.edu/(G1)/guides/rs/sat/img/cir.rxml
Color Enhanced Infrared Images, University of Illinois.

Index